DEC 14 2018

My Beauti...
Susie ~
What can I say
I saw this and thought
of you — one of the best
Badass GRRLZ I knew
Love ya lady
Happy Solstice
xx Elle

# The Badass Girl's Book of Prayers

*For Girls with Soul, Sass and a Lot of Badass*

Maimah Karmo and Tania Koulakian

BALBOA
PRESS
A DIVISION OF HAY HOUSE

Copyright © 2018 Maimah Karmo and Tania Koulakian.

All rights reserved. No part of this book may be used or reproduced by any means, graphic, electronic, or mechanical, including photocopying, recording, taping or by any information storage retrieval system without the written permission of the author except in the case of brief quotations embodied in critical articles and reviews.

Balboa Press books may be ordered through booksellers or by contacting:

Balboa Press
A Division of Hay House
1663 Liberty Drive
Bloomington, IN 47403
www.balboapress.com
1 (877) 407-4847

Because of the dynamic nature of the Internet, any web addresses or links contained in this book may have changed since publication and may no longer be valid. The views expressed in this work are solely those of the author and do not necessarily reflect the views of the publisher, and the publisher hereby disclaims any responsibility for them.

The author of this book does not dispense medical advice or prescribe the use of any technique as a form of treatment for physical, emotional, or medical problems without the advice of a physician, either directly or indirectly. The intent of the author is only to offer information of a general nature to help you in your quest for emotional and spiritual well-being. In the event you use any of the information in this book for yourself, which is your constitutional right, the author and the publisher assume no responsibility for your actions.

Any people depicted in stock imagery provided by Getty Images are models, and such images are being used for illustrative purposes only.
Certain stock imagery © Getty Images.

Print information available on the last page.

ISBN: 978-1-9822-1233-9 (sc)
ISBN: 978-1-9822-1232-2 (hc)
ISBN: 978-1-9822-1234-6 (e)

Library of Congress Control Number: 2018910994

Balboa Press rev. date: 09/28/2018

# CONTENTS

Why the Badass Girl's Book of Prayers ....................................................... ix
Badass Girl's Book of Prayers Foreword .................................................. xiii

With Every Breath You Take, Pray ............................................................. 1
Start With One Thing .................................................................................. 4
A Prayer to Relish Your Freedom .............................................................. 6
A Prayer to Know Your God-liness ........................................................... 8
A Prayer to Give Yourself the Gift of You! ............................................. 10
A Prayer for Becoming Vulnerable to the Process of Life .................... 13
A Prayer for Setting Intention for the Day ............................................. 15
A Prayer for Recognizing that You Are Pure Awareness ..................... 17
A Prayer to know that You are a Blessing to Others ............................. 19
A Prayer of Harmony to All Beings ......................................................... 21
A Prayer for Letting Go Into The Grace of God .................................... 23
A Prayer for When You Don't Know What the Fuck is Happening ....... 25
A Prayer for Staying On Path ................................................................... 27
A Prayer to Smash the Shit out of Your Day .......................................... 29

A Prayer to See the Divine Within ..................................................31
A Prayer to Step Fiercely Into Your Power .....................................33
A Prayer to Let go of Fear ...............................................................35
A Prayer to Experience Spiritual Surrender ...................................37
A Prayer to Allow Surrender Be Your Song ..................................39
A Prayer to Indulge in the Freedom of Being Alive ......................41
A Prayer to Honor Your Stillness ...................................................43
A Prayer to Know You Are The Source ........................................46
A Prayer to Become the Flame of God ..........................................48
A Prayer to Create Change in a World of Chaos ..........................50
A Prayer to Know that You are Loved! ..........................................52
A Prayer for Embracing Change .....................................................54
A Prayer for Eternal Happiness ......................................................55
A Prayer for Fearless Peace .............................................................57
A Prayer for Finding Forgiveness in Your Heart ...........................59
A Prayer to Help Let Go to the Flow of Nature ............................61
A Prayer to Unleash Your Wild ......................................................63
A Prayer for the Cove of Your Heart .............................................66
A Prayer to Help You Stay True To Yourself ................................68
A Prayer to Let Go of Judgment Today .........................................70
A Prayer to Bless the Flow the Life ................................................72
A Prayer to Open up to the Universe .............................................75
A Prayer to Look Beyond the Surface and Find Your Deeper Truth ........77
A Prayer to Tell Life What You Want It To Be .............................80
A Prayer for Activating the Flow of Abundance ...........................82
A Prayer for Awakening to Your Bliss ...........................................84
A Prayer to Look Within ................................................................86
A Prayer for Creativity ....................................................................88
A Prayer to Help Collaborate with Others ....................................90

| | |
|---|---|
| A Prayer to Know that You Are Perfection! | 92 |
| A Prayer to Inspire the Light Within to Glow and Flow Out | 94 |
| A Morning Prayer for a Fresh Start | 96 |
| A Prayer for you to Make Up Your Mind | 98 |
| A Prayer to Know that God is building you… | 100 |
| A Prayer to Honor the Struggle | 102 |
| A Prayer to Inhale and Exhale, Mindfully | 106 |
| A Prayer to Find Beauty in Life | 108 |
| A Prayer for Knowing God | 110 |
| A Prayer to Know That You Are Limitless | 112 |
| A Prayer for Unveiling your Light | 115 |
| A Prayer to Awaken the Divine Feminine in You | 117 |
| A Prayer to the Womb of Compassion | 119 |
| A Prayer to Deepen Your Experience of Gratitude | 121 |
| A Prayer to See the Beauty in your Everyday Life | 123 |
| A Prayer for Blessings | 125 |
| An Authentic Prayer for the Day | 127 |

# WHY THE BADASS GIRL'S BOOK OF PRAYERS

### Introduction by Maimah Karmo

If you're like most girls I know, you are a badass. You work hard, you play even harder, you smash your goals, and then you repeat. You want to make the world a better place, but you'll let someone know what's up in a second if they threw you some shade. You love Oprah and you're all "yasss, girl" when you see inspiring quotes on Instagram. You're also all kinds of zen, with a sprinkle of "don't play with me or I WILL cut you". In other words, you're just like us - a bit of Deepak and a bit of Tupac.

My life is pretty badass. I'm a badass, my friends are badasses, and we do badass things. We are also very spiritual, and rely on our connection with something bigger than us to guide and sustain us as we navigate our human selves, relationships with friends, family, children, and people we do business with, how we relate in the world, and how we show up and contribute to society every.single.day. Almost every successful woman I know has a foundation grounded in prayer. We need prayer. The more badass you are and the more hustle you've got, the deeper you need to focus on building and nurturing a relationship with whatever it is that you call God. As a woman, your wisdom extends from within the home where you provide counsel to family and friends, then outwards to those you may mentor and work with. Your energy, spiritual countenance, and words and deeds are the foundation upon which community and nations are built. You have a special power - and whether you believe it yet or not - you are a creator who creates the world around you. So, that connection with Spirit, through prayer is essential. It doesn't make you builds your sass, it gives you strength. It is your superpower. It is OUR superpower. It's also our armour. The deeper our relationship with Spirit Energy, the more capable we are to show up and manifest badass shit in the world.

So, that is why I pray constantly - because my ass needs it. My dreams depend on it. My soul is fed by it. Others I come into contact with, experience a better me because of it. I pray first thing in the morning, I whisper prayers to myself or read them throughout the day, and I wrap my day up at the end with a prayer of thanks and release. Sometimes I just talk to God about my desires, or I rant - it all depends on which mood I'm in. When I'm in Deepak mode, I imagine myself praying in a calm, centered, yogi or spiritual-like way. Other times when I'm frustrated and angry, I'm like, "fuck, fuck, fuck, fuck, fuck!!!!!! God, why the hell is this shit happening to me. I'm begging you, make this motherfucking shit fucking stop! Oh, and thank you God...and I'm sorry for cursing at you.......but for real, a sister needs a break. Love ya, G."

So, Tania and I wrote this prayer book in the spirit of keeping it real. You'll find prayers that make you feel all kinds of zen-warm-fuzzy ish, channeling your inner Oprah' & Deepak and there are some prayers for the days for when you're feeling like you have a little more in common with Tupac, Ice Cube or even The Terminator. You might also want to try reading some of the prayers in a Samuel Jackson voice.

But seriously, what I know for sure is that prayer is a deeply individual act. It is a relationship that you have with "All there is". Each of us can cultivate that relationship - between our self and Higher Energy. Prayer is poetry. It is how you express all parts of yourself authentically, while connecting with the Divine. Prayer is life. How you manifest in life is a prayer. Your life is a prayer. No one can define what that looks like for you. At the end of the day, how you talk to your God, Creator or Higher Power should be about authentic self-expression. If anyone tells you otherwise, they can go fuck themselves. Sending love and light...

Namaste,
Maimah and Tania

# BADASS GIRL'S BOOK OF PRAYERS FOREWORD

By Catherine Odderstol

You are an endless soul here in human form, pre-determined to move through the experience of life to remember who you really are, to remember you are connected to all that is, to remember that *love is all that is*. Here to recognize your unique heart drum beat in the symphony and to play it with courage - loud and proud!

Finding that beat may be the most difficult challenge of life. We humans are creatures of habit and routine. We *like* programming. And we have been riding the wave of technology, status quo, convenience, and conformity to the tune of a much lower frequency than that in which the truth of our Spirit abides.

We tend to believe we are the culmination of our thoughts and experiences, but that is limited. We are *not* limited. We are abundant, Divine, one with all of life. We are magnificent, powerful, capable, and creative. We are Creators. The mind can be a blank slate. Life can be a blank slate.

Every day can be a blank slate. Every moment is an opportunity to create and to resonate in the highest frequency that is your Truth.

Prayer and Mantra is your script – You are the author. Prayer and mantra are the repetition of your script – the new programming you crave to create the life you desire –the truth already beating in your heart. Thoughts vary in quality and carry certain frequencies, each unique thought with its own frequency. The highest thought frequency resonates in LOVE.

I admire your courage to create a new routine, and to decide to reprogram your reality, your story to the tune of Love, to your Truth. You are an endlessly badass soul and we *all* need each other to get into our grooves, to raise the collective frequency, to be our best selves, and to light this shit up!!!

# WITH EVERY BREATH YOU TAKE, PRAY

Prayer is not only something that you do kneeling by the bed bent in supplication.

Prayer is not only something you do with others in a church.

Prayer is not only isolated to what you utter at specific times.

Prayer is constant. Prayer is a practice. Prayer is the way.

Prayer is bold, brave and supernatural.

Prayer is tapping into the invisible realms, garnering the strength of your angels, guides and Higher energy sources and power.

Prayer is direct, divine communication with God, whatever your God may be.

Prayer is manifestation.

Prayer is creation.

Prayer gifts breath to your thoughts.

Prayer gives life to your beliefs.

Prayer unleashes your divine badass.

Prayer is your armour and your sword.

Prayer is the energy that calls forth the answer.

Prayer is the vehicle through which you express your divine self.

Instead of worrying, you bless the moment instead. That is another way to pray.

When you are mindful about your mindset in the moment - that is how you pray.

When you show love and compassion to others - that is how you pray.

When you use your life as a means of service – that is how you pray.

The thoughts you focus on – that is how you pray.

When someone wrongs you and you retaliate with authentic kindness – that is how you pray.

When things don't go your way and you bless the outcome – that is how you pray.

When you feel anxious or overwhelmed – stop and create silence – that is how you pray.

When you have faith in the midst of struggle – that is how you pray.

When you believe in God, even when you can't see the road ahead – that is how you pray.

A prayer is a promise.

A prayer is a wish.

A prayer is surrender.

A prayer is eternal.

A prayer is a deep, intimate and abiding communication with God.

With every breath you take… pray.

# START WITH ONE THING

Sometimes life can seem overwhelming, with so much to do.
Here's what I want to tell you…
**Start with one thing.**

When you wake up in the morning, and the first thing on your mind
is an endless list of tasks, and you don't know where to start.…
**Start with one thing.**

When you are trying to be the best parent, and have a long list
of things to pick up for your children, or doctor appointments
and sports to get to, don't think about it all at once.…
**Start with one thing.**

When you've made mistakes in your relationship or realize
that you've drifted apart, but it seems like there is too
much to fix and not enough time… think about a kiss or a
simple gesture of kindness… **Start with one thing.**

When you realize that you've made others a priority and you look in the mirror to realize that you need to get yourself in order, know that you don't need to do it all at once…
**Start with one thing.**

When you feel depressed, sad, or broken and you think that you're trapped and can't see your way out from under the sadness… take one step at a time towards the light…
**Start with one thing.**

When you begin to experience a big shift and you start to realize how great you are, how magnificent, bold, brave, special, unique, magical and beautiful you are, and are ready to change everything about the way you've been thinking and transform your life…
**Start with one thing.**

When you look at all that we have to do and be in life, it may seem like a lot, but if you focus on the present moment you can accomplish a lot by taking life one thing at a time.

Start today with one thing – love – for yourself, others and all of life…
**for you are your one thing.**

# A PRAYER TO RELISH YOUR FREEDOM

Beloved, in this moment, *recognize and relish your freedom.*

**Embrace** the freedom of expressing your unique and powerful existence.

**Release** identities and attachments that separate you from the truth of who you really are.

**Recognize** your real self, the one without the restrictions of your mind.

**Know** that you can choose to be liberated from the hypnosis of conditioning, fear and illusion.

**Notice** your desire to be all that you are - fan its flames, ignite the fire of change - to eradicate that which you are not.

**Be fully aware** about the phenomenon of your existence.

**Bathe** in your Infinite Nature.

**Allow** yourself to be overcome with bliss.

**Let go** of logic and intellect, and experience the wonderment of deep grace yearning to be discovered.

**Detach** from the 'self' that embodies fixed thoughts, learned behaviors and undying habits.

**Acknowledge** your human challenges, as opportunities that have the power to lead you to discover your Divine Nature.

**Have the strength** to surrender to the cosmic unfolding of consciousness.

**Rest in being**, where all is fresh and steeped in joy.

Open your heart to trust and faith so that you may experience the glory of effortless living.

Recognize, relish, release…be free.

## A PRAYER TO KNOW YOUR GOD-LINESS

As you embark upon this day that God has made,
I pray that you know in the depths of your heart, you
are a uniquely created manifestation of God.
I pray that you know that God, The Universe, and
eternity, all desire to be expressed through you.
I pray that you know legions of angels carry you, so that
nothing which forms against you will prosper.
I pray that you know you are protected –
in and out, and all around your being.
I pray that every memory of your past is loosened and let go.
I pray that you open your mind to the newness of this day,
to new things and people, to a new you.
I pray that you see God in everyone you meet.
I pray that you authentically express your "God-ness" in every
transaction and interaction with every person, place or thing.

I pray that you know how sacred your life is so that you may
treat it and your body with love, honor and respect.
I pray that you revere each breath and each beat of your heart.
I pray that you know how beautiful, magnificent,
special, wonderful and unique you are.
I pray that you know all you desire has already come true – trust in that.
I pray that if your plans do not come to fruition, you know God has
something even more magnificent and wonderful planned for you.
I pray that you move with passion throughout your day.
I pray that you move with purpose – purposefully
embracing the sweetness in every moment.
I pray that you take pause throughout the day
to tell yourself how wonderful you are.
I pray that you know you don't have to struggle.
I pray that you know you've already won.
I pray that light, love, peace, understanding and
joy infuses every aspect of your day.
I pray that you know you are loved to infinity and beyond.

Amen

# A PRAYER TO GIVE YOURSELF THE GIFT OF YOU!

**Today,** as you welcome this new day, slowly **inhale; then exhale.**

Give yourself a gift.

**Give yourself the gift of you.**

Take a moment and look into the mirror. **Intentionally, deeply and lovingly**…look at you.

As you look at yourself, **appreciate** the crown that is your hair. Know that every strand was loved and formed by God.

Look into your eyes, honor these beautiful windows to your soul that allow you to view the miracle of life.

Appreciate all that you set your sights on today.

May you send love to everyone you see. May your eyes emit **empathy, kindness, strength, and fearlessness;** may they send their magical, invisible light to surround anyone who may be feeling lonely, scared, worried.

May the power of your gaze set each individual you see on a trajectory of **healing, energy and buoyancy.** Let God's all encompassing love flow through your eyes and touch every living thing.

Hold your neck high and your shoulders straight. Pull up from the base of your spine all the way up, *kings and queens.* Remember that you are of royal heritage.

**You were beautifully, lovingly, patiently and meticulously formed.** Stand tall and remember that you are majesty.

I pray that you take a moment to send love, light and appreciation for every vertebrae, every muscle, every sinew that holds up your carriage. **You are the shit. Act like it.**

I pray that you know today who the heaven you are.

Now, send your focus to your core, hold it tight and firm. Feel the strength of your glutes, legs, your calves and your feet. Slowly, send love to every inch of those parts of your body. **Feel the powerful energy and life force run through you.** Know how much power resides in those parts of your body – enabling you to move throughout your day. Every step you take is **beautifully coordinated** by every part of your body. All coming together in concert, filled with life!

Take a look at your beautiful hands. Appreciate all the wondrous things that they do! They allow you to wash and bathe, cook, clean, touch and feel, nurture, love and hold the ones you love. Your hands allow you to open and close doors, drive, fold, they allow themselves to be folded in prayer. With them, you can caress your loved ones' cheeks. Open your hands – **and welcome all the blessings and bounties of life.**

Now, close your eyes and **imagine a ball of light** – as big as possible, yellow, white and violet colors, all swirling together. Imagine that this light encompasses all the wonderful feelings that you've ever felt and can imagine. Imagine that this light is re-invigorating. This light should excite you; calm you; soothe your soul. It's gets closer and closer. Now, it envelopes all of you, from the crown of your head to the soles of your feet. **You are the light. You are renewed, now,** in every way.

Now go, into the world, and share your love, your light and your healing energy with everyone you meet.

**You are light. You are love. You are life.**

**God lives in you.**

**Amen**

# A PRAYER FOR BECOMING VULNERABLE TO THE PROCESS OF LIFE

A seed is planted into the soil of the earth.

With the forces of nature and grace, the seed becomes vulnerable to all of the processes of becoming one day a grand tree that flowers the most fragrant of flowers.

It bears its fruits but does not hold on to them. The tree allows all who come across it to enjoy the fruits of its maturity.

Could I be like a flower?

Could I be like a tree?

Could I become empty enough to lessen my 'self' so that
I may experience life at its fullest potential, so I may too,
one day flower, exuding the fragrance of grace.

Could I become vulnerable enough to the whole process of life
so that all of my efforts in life not only affect the ones I call my
beloved but all who comes across the fruits of my labour?

May my roots be like a tree's, strong and sturdy.

In the balancing act of life, may my branches extend far
past my identity so that I may not only make a home for
myself, but all those in search for truth and liberation.

May my fragrance be like the fruit of the spirit, full
of love, joy peace, compassion and blissfulness.

May my self-image be just like the surface of a body of water, a
playing of light, dancing, ever-changing, malleable and clear.

Who knows where the earth ends and where it begins?
May I dissolve into the unknown.
May I dissolve into grace.

# A PRAYER FOR SETTING INTENTION FOR THE DAY

As I open my eyes, take my breath and feel my spirit awaken this beautiful, majestic, body of mine, I give thanks to God, the Universe, the angels and all love that supports my breath.

As I bathe, I wash away all that doesn't serve my highest good.

As I dress, I imagine myself shrouded in royal garb, girded with strength, enshrined with passion, shielded by love.

As I nourish my body, I fuel it with nutrients that enrich every molecule in my body, from the top of my head to the soles of my feet.

As I prepare to step out of my home, I take a moment to pause. With intention, I imagine a yellow light, grow within me, getting bigger and more powerful, until it surrounds me and imbues strength, protection and godliness, within all parts of me.

As I make my way into the day, may I shine the light of God upon everyone I meet. May I see the light of God in everyone I meet. May I give the light of God to everyone I meet – in all that I am, all that I say, and all that I do.

**Amen**

# A PRAYER FOR RECOGNIZING THAT YOU ARE PURE AWARENESS

Beloved,

Take a moment to observe your surroundings.
With your eyes, see all that is around you.
With your nose, smell all that is around you.
With your ears, hear all that is around you.
Observe.
Observe what begins to arise out of the body.
Observe what begins to arise out of the mind.
Simply Observe.
Be silent in your Observation.
Whatever arises, allow it.
Try not to attach to it in any way.
Become aware of it as it is.
A sensation, arising.

With full attention observing these sensations,
begin to see these sensations slowly subside.
Come to the understanding that all that arises, also subsides.

My wish and blessing for you today is to
watch
see
observe
hear
smell
taste
touch
with full attention
without attachment
and with great appreciation and contentment.

~Blessings and Love~

# A PRAYER TO KNOW THAT YOU ARE A BLESSING TO OTHERS

Today, my prayer for you is that you don't pray for you....

Instead, pray to be a blessing to others.

We often have our hands open in yearning, wanting, asking, desiring, begging for ourselves.

This is not what your Source desires.

Source energy and "All that is" emits all it is to life.

You were born filled with Spirit…

…and when you live with Spirit and are filled with spirit…

You are a walking manifestation and pouring out of God.

Your work is to pour those blessings onto others….

…to fill them, to lift them, to catapult them and transform them, so they may rise.

Let your prayer be this, "I will serve and bless others with what has been given to me".

Let your prayer be, "I will show infinite love to others".

Let your prayer be, "I will pour out the purest of love from my soul to uplift others with my presence."

Let your prayer be, "I will honor every human. I will honor every life".

Let your prayer be, "I will be of service to the other, before myself", for there is no "other", only extensions of myself in other bodies, for we are but one. In blessing others, we bless the whole, and in turn bless all of life."

# A PRAYER OF HARMONY TO ALL BEINGS

May all beings be happy.
May all beings be bright.
May all beings know their born sacred right to live a full life, regardless of race, gender, class or fight.
May all beings know life beyond time and space.
May all beings know peace.
May all beings know joy.
May all beings sit comfortably on the throne of awareness, filled with grace.
May all beings be equal.
May all beings know love.
May all beings be surrounded by compassion from above,
and from below because God has no direction,
everything we is just a pure reflection.
May all beings feel gratitude.
May all beings be wise.

May all beings be pure.
May all beings be clear.
May their minds be used as just a tool of joy and not as tools of fear.
May all beings imagine a day when we are awakened to the pureness of our very existence and know that nothing real and true can ever be taken.
May all beings connect and find harmony,
letting go from their hearts greed and jealousy.
May all beings know that love is everywhere,
there is nothing alive that didn't come from the creator itself.
May all beings know they are creators too,
and what they create is up to them and that they have the right to choose.
May all beings be strong in the pursuit of their true heart intentions.
May we build a safe and better world that includes all beings, even the ones they don't like to mention.

May we spread joy.
May we spread peace.
May we spread harmony.

# A PRAYER FOR LETTING GO INTO THE GRACE OF GOD

When along your path you find yourself at a crossroads, find a deeper silence and let go into the grace of God.

Let go and connect with the 'I' that is without identity. The "I" that is the Ultimate Truth, beyond the 'I' that you are attached to.

Disentangle from the branches of the mind's identity and conditioning. Release your hold on identity and reach instead for grace.

Living in fear, worry or doubt is not truly living. When you live in this place, you are stuck in the past or a hypnotic fear of the future.

In order to let go into the Grace of God, we must transcend our limitations and open up to the possibility of knowing the true Self, the 'I' of our being-ness.

Dear 'I' of being-ness: Although I don't know you and all of your glory yet, I am ready with openness to feel what resonates with my heart.

Through this openness may I fall into your Love. Naturally my eyes will open to what brings joy, what brings peace, and what brings space. There, in full illumination of the authentic 'I', I let go into the Grace of God and immerse into the collective to become One Being, alive-ness, being-ness, Truth.

# A PRAYER FOR WHEN YOU DON'T KNOW WHAT THE FUCK IS HAPPENING

God, I woke up today and my first thought was, "What the fuck is happening with my life right now?"

I feel like things are falling apart, like I'm falling apart and I can't quite seem to get back to myself.

God, I'm doing everything I can. I work hard. I do my best for others. I'm kind to my family and friends, I'm a really good person.

I don't understand why everything is so fucked up lately.

As much as I try, I find myself feeling sad, tired, unmotivated and unsure of who I am, scared of life in general. I want to curl up in bed and sleep all the time, not workout, eat, drink wine and not even smile. God, I think I'm depressed. Actually, I know I am. Sometimes, I don't know if I want to be here anymore. Life is too hard. Why is life so hard, God. Was it something I did?

What happened to me, God? I used to feel happy a lot of the time.

What happened to me God? I used to be a badass. I was Superwoman.

What's happened to me God? I used to be fearless. I thought I was a unicorn. I used to shit rainbows and butterflies. I used to rock life.

Lately, I don't feel like me, God.

Tell me what I need to do.

Tell me how I need to be.

God, please give me an answer.

God, I don't know WTF is happening or why.

Can you help?

God?

# A PRAYER FOR STAYING ON PATH….

Recently, I was at a retreat and went for a walk. I was on a path that wound around bushes and streams of water.

I could see my destination between the leaves of the trees. Sometimes there was so much foliage in the way that I couldn't see where I was going, but I knew that something beautiful was at the end because someone had mentioned this to me.

As I walked, the sun would beat down brightly allowing me to be confident in my steps. Then at times, the clouds would cover the sun or the terrain would change. I remained unwaveringly confident in where I was going, and stayed "on the right path".

As human beings, we like to plan. We like to be sure that we will have a life we choose. We want to know that if we do what we think is the right thing, the things we expect will come back to us.

When they don't, we feel that we are off path.

That's not the real truth.

The real truth is that you are always going the right way.

Instead of thinking you've veered off path, focus on your vision on life, focus on your feeling, focus on your alignment with what you desire in your heart, even when you don't see it with your eyes.

When the clouds come, let them.

When branches cover the sun's gaze, allow them.

Refuse to be intimidated by life.

Refuse to be afraid of getting lost.

Often times, it is in the getting lost that we truly find the way.

Walk in faith, and expect the unexpected… and know that with God, you are always on the right path.

# A PRAYER TO SMASH THE SHIT OUT OF YOUR DAY

Today, my prayer for you is to decide to smash the shit out of today.

Today, tell yourself, "Good morning, I am the bomb ass, boss queen, and I will conquer this motherfucking day."

As you get ready for your day, tell yourself, "My mind is clear. I am focused. I am already victorious over whatever the day brings."

Tell yourself, "I am prepared. My will is strong. My heart is ready. My body will carry me where I need to go."

Imagine yourself as a superhero or a badass biker chick, blazing into the day, surrounded by your supernatural support team - your warrior angels.

Imagine yourself stepping into your day like JLo, Beyonce, some RiRi, and a dash of Tina, Ertha and Cher. Every door will open for you. Every eye will await your next move. Every word spoken about you will be for you. Today, expect a "yes" to every request you make.

Whatever you goals are - today and in the future - believe that they are already done. Let go of the pressure and waltz into your day like a queen.

As you go over your to-do list, claim that victory has already been won.

Today, decide to stop living in two other worlds that don't serve you - the past and the future, because in the straddling of these two worlds, you lose sight of the present view.

Go into your day, not worrying about how you will do it all, but with the assurance that it is already handled.

Decide to let go of limiting beliefs around time, money, age and circumstances in your life.

Today, you will claim what you're worth — change what you think, what you say and what you do.

Today, you will decide to discover another part of yourself — the part of you that you dream of being — and stop thinking "if only I could".

Today, you will do a great thing, because you are a great thing.

Today, you will knock your life out of the ballpark. Smash the shit out of your goals. Embrace the abundance that awaits your day.

# A PRAYER TO SEE THE DIVINE WITHIN

Today, you will see the divinity within, because you are Divine.

Today, you will remember that you hold the genetic makeup of the Creator. Bliss is your birthright. Unleash your light within.

Today, you will decide to have compassion for yourself.

Today, you will decide to exercise your life for good.

Today, you will allow God to do the "impossible" through you.

Today, you will decide to allow God to walk ahead and prepare a place for you.

Today, you will remember that the church starts within.

Today, you will know that you never fail.

Today, decide that you will only live in light and truth – awakened and fully present to it all.

Today, decide to stop pursuing life, but instead, allow your soul to express in life.

Today, recognize that you are divine.

# A PRAYER TO STEP FIERCELY INTO YOUR POWER

As you blossom into your power this can cause a reaction from others who are not ready to walk the same path as you.

Step into your power and don't ever look back.

I pray that if others actions towards you originate from fear, insecurity, jealousy or anger, that you do not take it personally. Everyone comes from their own place. Mind your own business and focus on you.

Allow others to be on their own paths of healing and tune into what's going on in your life. Perhaps they could be a mirror of you… perhaps it's time for you to change a pattern as a result. Whatever you do, acknowledge the lessons, acknowledge the blessings, and step into the power of you.

I pray that you know that vulnerability is your greatest shield against self-judgement and self-hate.

I pray that you sit in the fire of your heart and reflect unconditional strength, protection and security. Your loving embrace and unapologetic outlook on life will bring forth the wisdom of your heart where the pure fire of peace burns eternally inside of you.

Own your divine light and let it burn bright! May you spread this fire through all beings that you encounter so that they too, can ignite from the light of the eternal flame of love.

Choose love today. Step fiercely into your power.

# A PRAYER TO LET GO OF FEAR

In reflection, clear your mind and look into your heart.

Are there fears that are holding you back?

Give them gratitude for how they may have protected you, and let them go.

Are there judgements, blockages that stay locked deep within?

Bring them to conscious awareness and give them permission to go.

Is there a part of yourself that you don't want to face because there is too much effort required?

Envision light around your heart. This light is effortlessly doing work… Cleansing and releasing. Become conscious of your breath. Feel your breath circulating through your body, working with the light, allowing it to flow everywhere your breath goes. The fear is letting go.

Is there shame that you are hiding, that is weighing you down?

Step into the feeling of the aliveness of your soul. In that place, there is no place for anything that does not help or heal you. All that is not you will begin to subside as you bring yourself back to your true nature which is at peace with what is, and letting go of what is not.

Are there people with whom you share personal space and time, who may be holding you back from staying aligned with the truth of your soul?

Step into your strength now, and address the areas of your relationships that require you to speak your truth, regardless of what others believe. By acknowledging and respecting your right to be real, you open space for others to do the same. You may grow together or apart, but know that whatever the outcome may be, it is for the greater good. Let go into this awareness now.

Are you experiencing fear about the future?

You realize that you have no idea what the next minute, hour, day, month or year has in store. With fear and judgement of the unknown, you create a blockage that stays locked under your permission. Unlock the doors and let fear go.

Accept the mystery of life. Be guided by the presence of All That Is. Allow that presence to dissolve anxiety, blockages and fear.

Allow what is to come. Let go what is not real to go. Your fear can now be let go.

# A PRAYER TO EXPERIENCE SPIRITUAL SURRENDER

Take your hands off the wheel and **experience spiritual surrender.**

**Fear,**
I thank you for arising, as you help me to know that I am filled with my own strength and the strength of the universe.
**Guilt,**
I thank you for arising, as you help me become aware of where I have been holding onto emotions that prohibit me from experiencing my life to its fullest expression.
**Shame,**
I thank you for showing up, for you teach me to let go of illusions of my mind that keep me stuck in patterns that do not serve me.
**Grief,**
I thank you for showing up, for you teach me to recognize pain, yet strive to gracefully accept that which cannot be changed.

**Uncertainty,**
I thank you for arising because you help me to have faith in the timing of the universe.
**Doubt,**
Like a lotus flower in muddy water, I surrender all of my perceptions about life and allow my spirit to bloom. And in my existence, I radiate the utmost expression of beauty, peace, joy, truth, gratitude and **Love.**

**I experience full surrender to Spirit.**
*Amen*

# A PRAYER TO ALLOW SURRENDER BE YOUR SONG

Let surrender be your song.

For so many people, "surrender" is perceived as a weakness; embrace it as your strength.

Let surrender be your song.

Surrender all your visions, goals and plans to God. Sing with excitement that they are already fulfilled and complete. Sing songs of celebration.

Let surrender be your song.

Surrender all your cares, worries, and frustrations to God. Sing with joy that they have vanished away, melted into the ether, and that they all have been solved.

Let surrender be your song.

Surrender all your success, wins and triumphs to God. Sing with praise that they do not define you, but that you are defined by your relationship with all that is Higher than you. From the Universal goodness of all that is all, from which you have come.

Let surrender be your song.

Surrender your aches, pains, illnesses and frailties. Sing with a resolution that you are healed in a deep, eternal way.

Let surrender be your song. Surrender all the ideas of who you think and feel you should be. Then surrender more… to the magnificence, beauty and love that you are, surrender to that light. Sing a song of rebirth, of rejuvenation and of unity with all the magic that ever was and ever will be.

Surrender, my loves, and sing!

# A PRAYER TO INDULGE IN THE FREEDOM OF BEING ALIVE

Dear Self,

From the moment your eyes opened to the light of the world this morning, your new story began; bask in the freedom of being alive and starting again.

As you sit in the stillness of morning awakening, become aware of your body, become aware of your presence, become aware of your ability to move through life, to design, to create. You are alive! Jump and express your freedom to live!

As you move throughout your day, observe your actions. Become aware of which are part of the deepest you, and which are from the story written about you by your ego, by others; family, friends, work, society. Let go of the chains of this limiting identify. Break free and indulge in the freedom to be fully, freely you!

Beloved,

May you turn inward and understand that the way in which you
speak to yourself is an indication of what you believe about yourself.
Indulge in the freedom of a speech filled with only love for yourself.

May you become conscious of how you think about yourself,
and how your thoughts create all that is unfolding in
your life at this very moment. Indulge in the freedom to
manifest thoughts that create a joyful life for yourself.

May you become conscious of your relationship with creation,
and the freedom you have to collaborate with life.
In this loving relationship with life, choose to align with Divine action.
Tap into the this feeling of 'I AM' and 'I EXIST'.

Love,

Surrender to the feeling of limitless energy flowing through you.
Surrender to the illumination permeating you.
Surrender to the empowering presence illuminating you.
Simply be.

Alive.
Free.

# A PRAYER TO HONOR YOUR STILLNESS

My prayer for you today, is that you honor your stillness… for within stillness, we find God.

Today, I pray that at the moment you open your eyes, you pause to honor the time between sleep, and awakening.

I pray that you honor the divine space that cradled your spirit while you rested and restored your body while you slept.

Honor the time between there and now.

Honor the reincarnating, the creating, the manifesting, the healing, the awakening…. Honor the quiet between where your humanness was and where your soul is in this moment.

Before you get out of bed, honor God. Honor the spirit that breathed in and through you, even when you were unconscious and asleep.

Honor the transformation that occurred in your every cell, your bones, your muscles, every sinew, atom and marrow.

Honor the stillness between… the time between here and now.

Honor the stillness.

Pause… don't do.

Honor the being…your being…

Honor the God-ness within. Be strong enough to honor the quiet… to honor your soul… to honor the place from which you cometh… for you are out of this world….

Honor the power in the pause, to reconnect with the extraordinary existence that is your soul…

Go back to whence you cometh…and bring that with you into your day.

Remember that quiet place, the nothingness, the everything… the all…

Honor your God-ness, your divine, your "not normal", your paranormal being.

Honor your living with the only currency that matters…the currency of God, of love, of stillness… do not plan the next step, because this is the only step… the now.

Honor your stillness, honor your deep knowing, deep meaning, deep understanding that you'll find only in the stillness.

Honor your God-ness….. Stop. Be still. Communicate with your other worldness. Let it love you, let the quiet win.

# A PRAYER TO KNOW YOU ARE THE SOURCE

My prayer for you today is to know this… you are the source,

You are the source of love, so show love in all that you do.

You are the source of faith, so exemplify faith in all that you are.

You are the source of joy, so express pure bliss for all that you have.

You are the source of peace, so let your mind be still, letting go of any chaos that attempts to infiltrate your life.

You are the source of wonder, so always dream, wish and hope.

You are the source of uncharted voyages, let your world be unlimited by geography… you are land, air, sea, and beyond.

You are the source of purity, so breathe out any discord, and dissonance or doubt.

You are the source of service, so give more than you ask for.

You are the source of wisdom, so always reach for your highest thought.

You are the source of creation, so live in awareness of the power of your every manifestation.

You are the source of silence, *for in silence you hear God's every word.*

You are source. You are Universe. You are one with the Creator.

So go into the world and source….begin it…

Go into the world and verse…speak it…

Go into the world and create…manifest it.

# A PRAYER TO BECOME THE FLAME OF GOD

Become the flame of God. Allow the light of the most perfect to flow through you.

Become the flame of God. Let nothing that comes near you dim your glow.

Become the flame of God. Shine bright and strong, keeping out of the darkness.

Become the flame of God. Never be consumed by the darkness of doubt or fear.

Become the flame of God. Illuminate the way for others.

Become the flame of God. Blaze a path so brilliant that you can never be consumed by any other element.

Become the flame of God. Light within a spiritual awareness and warrior godliness – burn higher and higher.

Become the flame of God. Fill up with this light from the crown of your head down to the soles of your feet. See that your eyes, lips, fingers and legs are wonderfully alive, lit from the inside out with strength, love and power.

Become the flame of God. Allow God to use you for his purposes into eternity.

Tell yourself, "I am the flame of God, and my flame is my soul's promise to the world"

# A PRAYER TO CREATE CHANGE IN A WORLD OF CHAOS

Universe, you gave me my first breath and my last breath belongs to you.
You are my mother and my father and I feel
your nurturing embrace around me.
My surroundings come from your light and I am
interconnected with all that you have created.
I recognize that all beings on Earth are doing the best that they can.
They, too, are here for growth,
and therefore I move from judgment of others into total acceptance.
I honor their paths.
Universe, with your Infinite Intelligence you created the
beautiful diversity that exists on Mother Earth,
and therefore I recognize the wisdom of diversity.
I accept that there is no one right way but a never-ending
amount of ways to learn, grow and experience.
Some choose the way of pain and suffering, while
others choose a softer, gentler, more loving way.

With the glory of your grace, I become sensitive to your call
for reconnection to heal myself to all that surrounds me
I look at the paths of others only so that I may be better
aware of how I can serve humanity and Mother Earth.
I AM that I AM, all you have created me to be, and
I allow all that I can be to take expression.
Universe, I pray that all the world may find
peace. After all, we are all one spirit!
May we awaken to this truth and love and embrace one
another in all of our wonderful and uniquenesses.

*Amen*

# A PRAYER TO KNOW THAT YOU ARE LOVED!

At this moment, wherever you are, rest with assurance that you are loved by the greatest love of all.

At this moment, rest in belief that you were formed by the most powerful energy in the world. You were lovingly crafted by the energy of the same fabric that composes the grandest to the most minute detail of all that is.

At this moment, rest in the belief that you can stop seeking perfection, because you will never get THERE. Instead, be in the moment. Perfection is a journey to which there is no end. Be here NOW.

At this moment, rest in the knowledge that most of what you worry about will never happen.-Let all these untrue creations in your mind disintegrate, for they are only illusions.

At this moment, know for sure that every beautiful thing you can imagine, will come your way. You gently need to move into your attracting energy and out of your own way to manifest it.

At this moment, know that you are understood, appreciated and supported. God's arms are wrapped lovingly around you.

At this moment, let your anxieties fall away, imagine taking a shower, and watching them fall, drifting and draining away. Now you are new, fresh, clean, free of suffering.

At this moment, imagine you have the power to heal someone through your words. Express that love, give a hug, look at someone and let your eyes radiate all the wonderful things you are feeling and thinking. Serve to illuminate their being.

At this moment, forgive and know that you are forgiven. Like the leaves carried away by the water in a river, let all the anger, unforgiveness, and judgment you feel towards others drift away.

At this moment, know that you are a beacon of light for all that comes into your life. Others can feel the warmth and bask in your love before they even see you. You are a beacon of hope, a beacon of faith, a beacon of joy, a beacon of blessings for all whom you radiate upon.

At this moment, know that you are wonderful expectation. Expectation of constant transformation, good and wonder.

At this moment, know that this moment is all.
Be in it.

# A PRAYER FOR EMBRACING CHANGE

When I look at the world around me, I will choose to focus on not what I can't control, but embrace that it is always changing.

When my mind tells me I am afraid of change, I will focus on my heart and its beating as it is the requisite of change and flow of life.

When my emotions trigger me in a way that fills my body with anxiety, I will remind them that everything is in perfect alignment, that I can let life be, because without life's challenges I would not be able to grow and blossom into a magnificent being.

Today, I acknowledge the divinity of life and realize that I am not just flesh and blood, skin and bones, but I am the eternal Spirit.

As I shift my awareness, not even the fear of death can trouble me, as I know that too, is just a passage to change.

I embrace change.

# A PRAYER FOR ETERNAL HAPPINESS

At your purest form, you are eternal happiness.

At your purest form you bend towards a light that attracts all beings.

In clarity and pure awareness, sit in the seat of eternal happiness. Happiness is all that is true and real.

As human "beings", we have the opportunity to become aware and conscious "beings". Step into this potential of eternal happiness. Right now, you can begin.

*In clarity and pure awareness, sit in the seat of eternal happiness where all that is true and real never ceases to exist and that which is untrue and unreal never comes to form.*

Just like the waves of water playing on the ocean surface, the mind and emotions play in awareness itself, painting the landscape of life with different vibrations, colours, shapes and sizes. Settle into the joy that comes from the art of life.

*In clarity and pure awareness, sit in the seat of eternal happiness where all that is true and real never ceases to exist and that which is untrue and unreal never comes to form.*

You were never separate from pure joy to begin with. That belief was only an illusion. Now, let this flicker of awareness light a spark. Realize that you are joyous light, the whole fire.

*In clarity and pure awareness, sit in the seat of eternal happiness where all that is true and real never ceases to exist and that which is untrue and unreal never comes to form.*

At your purest form, you are eternal happiness.

# A PRAYER FOR FEARLESS PEACE

Take a seat in the stillness of your being where you are aware of all the thoughts, emotions, feelings and sensations arising in and around you. Observe from the place of awareness, the place of fearless peace.

Your thoughts may be agitated, fast, disorganized or rigid. Emotions may erupt with anger, sadness, confusion or despair.

But remind yourself you are the still one, the one who surrenders into fearless peace.

People around you, your community and the world as a whole will change, fluctuating with dramas and traumas.

But you are the still one, the one who surrenders into fearless peace.

Your old patterns may arise with a vengeance, wanting to take over your being without mercy or compassion. No matter the patterns or experiences, know this…

You beloved, are the still one, the one who surrenders into fearless peace.

When your finances decrease, expect bounty, fullness and increase…

You beloved are the still one, the one who surrenders into fearless peace.

In fearless peace and pure stillness, you are untouchable.

Nothing that takes place in your human experience can enhance or diminish your glorious awareness.

Remember always, you are the still one, the one who surrenders into fearless peace.

# A PRAYER FOR FINDING FORGIVENESS IN YOUR HEART

Dear Self, if you could know one thing, know that there are no mistakes.

In life there are only re-takes of experiences – do not allow judgement to creep in.

When people let you down, allow yourself to feel what you feel, but allow these thoughts and emotions to be temporary. Fleeting. They do not provide clear perceptions of people, places or things.

When hurtful situations occur, reach into a deep state of awareness and observation. In this place, you will be ready to sit with the universe at the center of your heart. This is where you will find forgiveness - within.

When you've been betrayed, allow your heart map lead you back to a place of truth. You cannot ever be betrayed by what is really meant for you.

When you feel that you have been invalidated, take the attention back from them and onto you. Close your eyes and feel the fire burning deep within your soul. You are not a coincidence. You were purposefully crafted. You live in grace. In this graceful place, find forgiveness within.

In any experience that does not honor you, know that you are vanquished. Imagine that time and space now separate yourself from that experience. Imagine it further and further away, then small as a pin prick, then as a speck, then disappeared.

Whenever you find yourself toughening up and becoming bristled by the hurt others bring, envision that those hardened beliefs and emotions have melted away. In this moment - release the unforgiveness. Reclaim your oneness in the Universe, and rest in the knowledge that you don't find forgiveness and compassion. You are that.

Allow your vibration to elevate to the frequency of mother earth. Let your vibration sing every song. Let your vibration elevate to the highest love, and let that love imbue every cell within you, and wish this healing for everyone on the planet – both the hurt and the healing.

In this space, be forgiveness, be healing, be light.

# A PRAYER TO HELP LET GO TO THE FLOW OF NATURE

Dear Self, take a look around you.
What do you see?
Is it all you wanted life to be?
Dear Self, take a look at yourself.
What do you see?
Are you all you wanted to be?

Dear Self, take the time to reflect.
Go a little bit deeper,
find the time to connect.

Dear Self, don't worry one bit.
Nature is here for you,
there is no need to stress.

Dear Self, breathe in the air.
Bless the oxygen that keeps you alive,
Have you taken the time to care?

Dear Self, I know it can be hard when the mind is occupied with thoughts.
But know that nature is always here to heal you when you're in a knot.

Dear Self, it's time to let go to the ideas you have about life,
Nature never wanted you to be left alone in midst of all your strife.

Dear Self, like the water in the river, just flow with the current called life
It will always bring you exactly where you need to be,
just tune in to find your deeper purpose,
there you will feel most alive!

# A PRAYER TO UNLEASH YOUR WILD

Good morning gypsy goddess boss. Today, unleash your wild.

Let go of the trappings of adulthood, let your hair down.

Release the ideals of being "put together". Allow yourself to be free.

Relish the skin you're in. Love your freckles, your moles, your hair, your quirks, your weirdness. Allow them to become your bling.

Embrace the sway of your hips and the strength of your thighs. Remember that wonder rests at the tip of your breasts. The world wets its lips every single time it meets you.

Embrace your wild. Imagine that you are barefoot, in the wild of nature, devoid of anything that makes you feel contained. Imagine that you are naked. Untamed. Running in the rain, wet and wild. You are a force to be reckoned with.

Embrace your wild. Embrace this moment. Between your legs and from within your womb, all that is on this Earth is birthed. Allow your inner Goddess to reign over her creation.

Embrace your wild. You dancing with fire. You are one with time. You are either and water.

You are laughter, and sacred.

You are naked truth.

You are effervescent force.

You are the rhythm of drums, throbbing pulsation of energy.

Your divine feminine summons the daylight.

At night, you howl at the moon.

You are intertwined with temples, jewels and treasures.

You are love.

You are light.

You are wild.

You are free.

You are the coitus.

You are ancestry.

You are the drums that pound and beat, as you reach your highest heights, and explode from the life force within.

Embrace your wild.

# A PRAYER FOR THE COVE OF YOUR HEART

Your heart is a magnetic cove, attracting all that you covet.

As you read these words, become aware of this feeling from your core.

Allow this feeling to carry you into a space
beyond your body and mind.

As a magnetic center, your heart is a great generator of energy and
life force which can manifest whatever it pulls into your orbit.

The magnet that is your heart is surrounded
by a peaceful heavenly lake.

A lake of love, warmth, contentment and peace.

Your heart attracts what is clear.

As your spiritual self drifts on this lake, the sparkle of the sun illuminates the water and reflects back onto you.

As you bask in peace and harmony, you begin to realize all of your hopes and dreams.
They are already with you, waiting for you to acknowledge them and commit to their manifestation.
Your heart is the soul's gateway, timeless and indestructible.
It contains all of the higher knowledge necessary to lift your physical, emotional, mental and spiritual self.

It is no coincidence that your physical heart is a tool to generate the vitality and strength needed to pump blood to all of your limbs and organs.
Your heart is what keeps you alive and thriving.
Your heart pulsates with strength.
Your heart is magnetic.
Your heart is silent and still.
Your heart is a sacred cove.
Your heart, is YOU.

May you know your true self in all of your heart's might.

# A PRAYER TO HELP YOU STAY TRUE TO YOURSELF

My prayer for you today is this….that you stay true to you, that you stay in intention with how you want to feel, in what you say and all that you do.

My prayer for you today is that you commit to conversing more gently, lovingly and deeply with yourself, to courting yourself, to discovering the unique and valuable gems that lay inside of only you.

I pray that every day you choose to embark with intention on a deeply spiritual and thoughtful journey with yourself…leading you to a more intimate relationship with your soul.

My prayer for you is that as you discover more of yourself, and expand your beautiful essence in the world, that you have the confidence to stay in your deepest truth. That you courageously and boldly stand in your unique place in the world, inspiring others to stand in their truth.

I pray that your spirit is centered, open and free, so that you can explore, enjoy and integrate the endlessness of your gifts, talents and imaginings.

My prayer for you is that you don't say "yes" when you want to say "no".

...that you don't stay when you want to go.

...that you know that one of the greatest gifts you could ever give yourself is the gift of digging deeply into yourself...

My prayer for you is that you are brave enough to follow the direction that best suits the vision for your life.

I pray that where you see mountains, they become "blessing" stones to higher ground...

I pray that where you see fear, you begin to see opportunities for fortune.

I pray that where you have tears, they shower to fertilize the ground beneath and before you, planting seeds for growth.

I pray that where you see anything as lacking, you know that you are already filled with flavor in every way.

Instead of shrinking away from what you perceive as unknown, I pray that you prepare your vessel to receive all the wonderment, bounty, success and flow that your vision has prepared as promised for you.

Stay true my loves, stay true.

# A PRAYER TO LET GO OF JUDGMENT TODAY

My prayer for you today is to have no more judgment for another or for yourself. This is one of the hardest things to do, but it must be done in order for us to live in full alignment with self and others.

Judgment is not kind. It does not have to be spoken to be felt. It is palpable and it keeps us separate from each other, and from one love.

Today, let go of it. No more judgment.

This means you must release any unkind ideas about yourself and your life. You must stop thinking of yourself as living in lack, being weak or powerless. You are abundant, strong, powerful and brave.

Release any ideas that you are not protected, that your foundation is not strong. You are secure and steady.

Release any critical thoughts of others, release any grudges, any judgments, any ideas of retribution. You are accepting, loving, forgiving, supporting and loving.

Release any negative judgment about the past, decisions, choices – whether in relation to yourself or to others. You are all doing your best.

Release the idea that they are wrong and that you are right. Every one of us is learning as we journey through life.

Release the idea that you are just a human being and that this is just life. You are a divine miracle.

Embrace that.

Let go of judgment.

Let go of separateness.

Let go of believing that it should be any other way than it is.

# A PRAYER TO BLESS THE FLOW THE LIFE

My prayer for you today is to focus your intention on allowing life to flow.

Take a deep breath in, and then exhale.

Do you feel that breath, that exchange of energy? That is flow. It is an allowance in followed by an act of letting go.

One of the biggest lessons we may come to terms with in this life, is that the only thing we can be certain about is that nothing is certain. Thus, we must stop fighting with the energies that be and their assistants, the winds of change. Change is a blessing that enables us to transform and grow. Transformation and growth are what we came here for. We choose or were chosen to incarnate in this space and time, to experience all of life.

Along the way, we forget our true "why". Caught up in life, we forget that we chose to come here to get caught up.

The trick is remembering that we are here to observe and participate… along with the millions of others that are also playing the game of life – of whom you have no control over.

The secret to more effortless living is to flow…. to allow experiences to come in and to allow them to flow out.

Today, appreciate all the wonderful things that come into your life. Tune into the frequencies of energy that surround you and all that you are. Bless the incoming flow.

Equally, if you are holding onto something that is causing you doubt, pain, anxiety or worry, let it go. Let it flow out of your life. That is the same with everything that disrupts your peace, your joy, and your health. Let old memories, limiting beliefs of yourself and others flow out of your life. Let ideas of what you can't do or be flow out of your life. Bless the outgoing flow.

Inhale, and breathe in and allow the inflow of alignment, of authenticity, of effortlessness, of everything you desire and more. Flow in good thoughts and behaviors. Flow in the intention to focus on only the people and things that help you vibrate higher. Bless the incoming flow.

Exhale and flow out that knot in your chest; flow out every blockage in your body and throughout your chakras. Flow out any negative past or present energy, pacts, promises or relationships. Bless the outgoing flow.

Flow in all the treasures of life, the beauty of the trees, blades of grass, the birds, butterflies, a touch, a smile, a kiss, a hug, a voice. Flow in what feels good. Flow in abundance and love. Bless the incoming flow.

Flow out distractions, contradictions, drama, chaos and strife. Flow out all that doesn't feel good. Bless the outgoing flow.

Flow in the expansion of your territory. Flow in the legend that you've already become. Flow in communion, understanding, protection, restoration, assurance and miracles. Bless the incoming flow.

Bless the incoming and bless the outgoing. Appreciate them both as the natural ebb and flow of life.

Bless the darkness and the light. Without one, there is no other.

Bless the flow of life.

# A PRAYER TO OPEN UP TO THE UNIVERSE

My prayer for you today is to open up.

Oftentimes we ask for something, but keep it to ourselves, holding that prayer quietly to our chest, putting our lives on hold until it happens… waiting for it to come true.

This is not how prayers come true. First you must open up.

You must open your heart and fill it with gratitude for what is.

You must open up your spirit to divine energy… you must open up to Source.

You must open up to your connection with all that is around you.

You must open your eyes to see the miracles that come your way.

You must open your mind to everything, no matter how small.

You must open your lips and speak your desires as your truth.

You must honor all that is manifesting for you.

You must open up to the Divine.

You must bless every experience.

You must allow every aspect of your body to be an eager vessel, excitedly waiting for the manifestation of your prayer.

You must open up to receive all that the Universe is working to bring to you.

# A PRAYER TO LOOK BEYOND THE SURFACE AND FIND YOUR DEEPER TRUTH

Today, I pray that you will look beyond…

Look beyond what people say and do… look deeper for their truth.

I am often asked by people as to why I am friends with this or that person, how is it that I have so many different types of friends.

The reason is simple… I look beyond.

People come to life with different experiences, varying lenses, and their own life contracts. They show up in our lives, often to teach us something, and if we don't like what they show up as, we ask ourselves, "how did they get here" or, "something must be wrong with them."

What I believe we need to do is look beyond what people say and do… or what they don't say or don't do.

We must look deeper, for their truth.

When you're near them, how do they vibrate? What does that tell you?

How does your soul feel about them and what they are in your life to do?

How are they being? Is it really about you? Or could you, by being you, serve as a transformation, a catalyst?

Look beyond what people do.

Behind every smile is a tear.

Behind every harsh word is a fear.

Behind every malicious word is self-doubt.

Behind every bully is a cover up.

Look beyond what people do.

Is there a pain that you could heal?

Is there a fear that you could help someone release?

Is there a shift that you could inspire in someone?

Is there new life awaiting to be awakened, that just needs your water and your sun?

Is there someone who's very life depends on your kindness and love?

Is there something different you could do or say?

You don't have to change people. Just look beyond what they do...

Accept...

Love...

Release Judgment...

While honoring your boundaries, be the light...

## A PRAYER TO TELL LIFE WHAT YOU WANT IT TO BE

Today, I pray that you tell life how you want it to be.

Oftentimes, we allow circumstances to become us. We allow things to happen to us, and we relinquish control of where we are going and who we are being.

Tell life how you want it to be.

In the stillness, quiet your mind and listen to your soul.

Know that any negative experiences you are having are not permanent, nor are they a promise of what's to come.

Tell your life what you want for it to be.

In the stillness of your mind, let go of all the feelings that are based on past experiences, and all the memories that want to convince you of how the future is supposed to be. Ignore them.

Tell life how you want it to be.

Tell yourself that you are a brilliant light, blissful and bursting, a beacon of peace, expansion, perfection, fulfilling and creating your wildest dreams.

Tell life how you want it to be.

That you have all that you want and need. That your joy shines through. That you are rare, beautiful and fragrant. That you illuminate everything in your path.

Tell life how you want it to be.

Tell life that you are secure and confident, calm and focused, that you walk with ease, that you are powerful and that creation flow through you.

Tell life how you want it to be.

That you are a masterful creator. That YOU really do it all.

Tell life how you want it to be.

Tell life that is is fun, that our mindset is really about what we set our minds on... what do you set your mind on being true for you?

Tell life how you want it to be…. Then be that.

# A PRAYER FOR ACTIVATING THE FLOW OF ABUNDANCE

When a seed is planted into the earth's soil, it takes many years for it to become a tree magnificently abundant with fruits and flowers. Without expectation it grows and grows until it is ripe for harvest. This tree however does not just grow on it's own, it is supported by all that nurtures it. The soil, water, air and the moon cycles. Even you, are a part of the tree's process on its journey to full growth and abundance. With this connection and pure oneness in mind, you are not alone. This process and deep connection comes from the vibration of deep compassion, love and gratitude. Beloved, allow yourself to rise into this energy field now and begin the process of activating the flow of abundance in your life.

With gratitude in your heart, begin to recognize the support around you, nurturing you towards your full growth and abundance.
With gratitude in your heart, allow the light of universal energy to fill you with joy and bliss.

With gratitude in your heart, begin to let go of negative thoughts and emotional patterns – all that hinders you from being embraced by the universal energies of deep compassion and love.

With gratitude in your heart, allow the nutrients of positive thoughts and emotions to flow through to your body, mind, and soul.

With gratitude in your heart, allow healing to take place in any area of your life that you feel deficient/needs some care.

With gratitude in your heart, allow divine grace to help you manifest the dreams that arise from your heart into this reality for not only your enjoyment but to share your fruits of success with those around you.

With gratitude in your heart, always remember that what you give will always come back naturally to you.

Beloved, open your heart to the flow of abundance now. Without fear or judgement, comparison or doubt, your life will flourish naturally, perfectly, blissfully.

# A PRAYER FOR AWAKENING TO YOUR BLISS

The universe is magical, filled with infinite opportunity, experiences, spontaneity, love and harmony.

I pray that you harness the Universe as yourself, unbounded with a natural ability to bloom and flourish into your fullest potential.

Each thing in nature - whether a teardrop or the sea - is comprised of the same thing, there is no separation.

I pray that you may have the vision to know the truth of your existence, Knowing that you are one with it all, because all is no-thing and everything all at once.

If we only analyze and label the world and people with our ideas,
We will never be able to know the essence of their souls.

I pray that you connect to your truest source internally and realize everyone that you encounter and connect with, are in your life for a soul purpose - to help shape you, heal you, transform you, and bring you back to unity.

No matter how many times the Universe tries to explain the truest nature of existence, it can truly never be put into words. What words can describe the magnificence and beauty of eternity?

I pray that you stay present to the beautiful mystery we call life and allow it to flow with ease.

Like a seed in the ground, the plant does not know what it will become, but behold a flower appeared, the most beautiful flower ever to grow from that tiny seed. That seed and that flower is you.

I pray that you find gratitude in all of your Awakenings to Bliss!

I pray that you always stay in your magic.

Awaken to bliss.

# A PRAYER TO LOOK WITHIN

Where do you look to find peace of mind?
I pray that you take the time and look within.
Where do you look to find happiness?
I pray that you take the time and look within.
Where do you look to find love?
I pray that you take the time to look within.
Where do you look to find wellbeing?
I pray that you take the time to look within.

When we look inside there are infinite possibilities for growth, expansion and evolution.
When we are constantly focused on the absolute truth of life, that this body and this mind will one day perish, we will not waste our time with mindless chatter and small gossip.
I pray that you focus on your divinity, the part of you that is infinitely capable for greatness, success, and grace.
I pray that you willingly pursue your freedom and find joy in all of your moments of "struggle", "resistance" and "limitation".

In those moments of darkness, I pray that with light feet, you tread the waters of your mind and sit in the jewel of your heart.

There you will find peace.
There you will find happiness.
There you will find love.
There you will find ultimate well-being.

# A PRAYER FOR CREATIVITY

These two eyes were meant to see all the beauty that surrounds me.

These two ears were meant to hear all the sounds of grace and its harmonies.

This nose was meant to smell the earth in all its glory.

This mouth was meant to taste all of the luscious tastes that nature provides.

These feet were meant to support me along my journey in this waking life.

These hands are an extension of my heart, manifesting all of my hopes and dreams.
If I gaze at my own reflection, I can see that this body, this mind has come from the earth, but my heart and soul is connected to the divinity in all beings in the whole entire cosmos.

With this divinity, I can create anything from my true hearts intent knowing that it is not me personally creating it, but the divine within.

I acquiesce to the force of nature flowing through my life and allow it to flow with ease and beauty.

# A PRAYER TO HELP COLLABORATE WITH OTHERS

Dear Partner,

I pray that in our collaboration, we bring the best of what we have to each other.

I pray that we freely give of our gifts, so that we elevate what the other brings.

I pray that we find a middle ground when we can't see eye to eye in our differences; knowing that our differences do not separate us, but bring the big picture closer together.

I pray that we can use our uniqueness to complement each other rather than compete.

I pray that we can accept each other for who we are, facets of the same shining light, illuminating our journey.

I pray that we bring joy to each other in the process and learn to laugh at each other's mistakes. When we point something that has the ability to enhance the other, it is taken with a lightness of heart.

I pray that when differences emerge, we will listen to each other with open ears and open minds.

I pray that we do not become defensive or close our heart to finding compassion in situation, that might seem dark.

I pray that we can heal each other with the words that we say.

I pray that every new day in our partnership is a chance to start all over again.

I pray that we can learn from each other, and become better together.

I pray that in every connection we grow like trees, branching out to create new arteries, planting new seeds, becoming extensions of each other's dreams.

I pray that in our collaboration, I support you as I support myself.

# A PRAYER TO KNOW THAT YOU ARE PERFECTION!

From this moment forward, my love, turn off the switch of believing that you are not good enough. From this moment on, shine the light on your perfection.

She Who Created All, laid in a bed of green grass, relaxed and soaking in in all of life and its bounty. As she took in the beauty all around her, she remembered that something was missing. That something was you.

She took her time. With love and care, she imagined you. She designed your image, she indulged herself, sprinkling stardust, moonlight, the sun and the stars in your cosmos. She formed you as a speck of light, then you grew and grew, from a droplet of desire, into the being that you now are. When you were born, the archangels heralded your coming. The birds sang in praise, the waters strummed as they ran over rocks, the ocean waved in excitement at the Earth. All creatures rejoiced. You had arrived. The world was now complete.

As you now are, you are perfect.

You are perfect as God sees you - not as as you see yourself; as a body, but as a beautiful spirit-filled abundant soul.

The mind works in such a way to analyze the world within and without. The mind tries to define the edges of existence with a sense of structure, but you have no structure. You are a work in motion. You are undefined. You are beautiful by no standard, because no standard can measure the brilliance of you.

Exactly as you now are, you are perfect.

As you look in the mirror and see your reflection, know that you are seeing God face to face. With the gentle gaze of love, with reverence, partake in all of life with grace - through the eyes of perfection. In any way that you think you are inadequate, render those thoughts non-existent. Know that you are united with Spirit.

In that union, you are perfect.

As you gain a deeper awareness, the true self is recognized. In this place, all peace and unconditional fulfillment thrives. Unconditional love vibes. Unconditional promise is wholeheartedly born over and over again. This is you at the very core.

In this delight, you are perfect.

## A PRAYER TO INSPIRE THE LIGHT WITHIN TO GLOW AND FLOW OUT

Light within, guide me home.
show me who I truly am.

Light Within, help me see,
help me be alive and free.

Light Within, show me love,
teach me what love truly is.

Light Within, point to the right path,
guide me straight to my bliss.

Light Within, ground my soul,
show me that I am already whole.

Light Within, make me silent.
teach me how to be in peace.

Light Within, I love you so.
 Thank you for all of your warmth.

Light Within, I allow you to Shine,
So the world around me can sense your warmth.

Light Within, I honor your truth,
knowing that we are united,
we are the same,
we are one.

# A MORNING PRAYER FOR A FRESH START

On this day allow yourself a fresh start.

On this day allow others a fresh start.

Release all past conclusions and future projections. Start fresh now.

Open your heart to the loving grace of the Universe and all its glory.

Wake up and recognize the first miracle today, that you are alive, breathing, healthy and conscious.

With this miracle in your heart, allow it expand into more miracles that give you more life.

Feel your heartbeat and know that through your heart you are connected to something far much greater than yourself.

With this connection in your heart, allow the limitless supply of abundance manifest in your life today.

May you be inspired by courage, kindness and compassion to be of service to yourself and all beings alike.

Blessings, Blessings, Blessings

On this morning, claim your fresh start; gift a fresh start to every relationship in your life; and everyone you meet.

# A PRAYER FOR YOU TO MAKE UP YOUR MIND

Today, here is my prayer for you. It is a prayer to diminish. It eradicates vacillation, rendering you resolute and unwavering about your vision.

My prayer for you is that you make up your mind.

Make up your mind to eliminate the pain of your past, and the fear that you might not get where you want to go.

Make up your mind, leaving no room for ifs, ands, or buts - only allowing room for getting to your goal.

Make up your mind, releasing wonder about the "how"; only setting your sights on the "when". In spiritual time and space...all you need to do is to be the pinpoint of that desire and soon, Earth time will catch up and get you there.

Make up your mind. Let nothing stand in your way.

Make up your mind. Then, you'll find that God is waiting for you, along with an army of angels, your spiritual crew.

Make up your mind to feel, say and be all that you were born to.

Make up your mind and be clear about your vision.

Make up your mind to finally know that God is on your side

Make up your mind to believe that fear will fall away, because it is only an illusion…

Make up your mind…. and you'll see that you've already arrived at where you desire to go.

# A PRAYER TO KNOW THAT GOD IS BUILDING YOU…

Have you ever seen a house being built? Not the kind these days where they put up houses in weeks, but a real house, where they set the foundation first, laying stones, waiting for them to settle, then building on that…

That is how God is building you.

Today, I hope you remember that God is building you, carefully, lovingly and with perfect precision and crafting.

He is building your foundation with good character, virtue, strength, love, hope, grace, peace, abundance, joy and steadfastness.

He equipped you with faith, understanding, perseverance, discernment and patience.

He decorated you with every experience, every person you meet, every laugh, every tear, every triumph, every fear.

He crafted you so that you can withstand every wind, any rainfall or storm.

He painted you with constant renewal and blessings, and blanketed you in peace.

As you go through life, with every experience, look to see how God may be using it to build upon what he created.

Know that he made only one of this house, only one of you, and put it high on the hill for all to see it's strength and its light, so that it inspires others to live as brilliantly.

# A PRAYER TO HONOR THE STRUGGLE

Today, I pray that you honor the struggle.

Yes, the struggle, for this is where you grow the most.

In each of our lives, there are times when we emotionally stumble and fall, sometimes we crawl, sometimes we curl into a ball, wounded, unable to move forward. Sometimes in life we think we are broken beyond repair, this is where we must pause and honor our growth.

We want to fix, we want to get through, we want to leap over the mountain of problems with money, love, work, children and self…yet, how do we learn, how do we overcome without the struggle. Pause and honor your growth.

You might have started the year strong and sure, confident and brave. You set your vision and were clear on where you were going, but then the challenges came at you like missiles. Like Wonder Woman, you dodged one and then the other. You leaped over the next obstacle, fell and despite your scapes, pushed over boulders, jumped over hurdles, yet the arrows, bullets and bombshells kept coming. You find yourself living in this struggle.

You might find that you gave up on your vision, yet your soul kept tugging at you, saying, "stay with me. Don't go to sleep."

You were tired.

You were scared.

You wanted to give up.

You barely felt alive anymore…but your soul whispered, "come on girl, let's go, you can do this. This is what warriors are made of. Let's go… you were made for this."

You struggled to your knees. You didn't recognize the "me" that you saw.

You wanted to bury your head in the sand.

There is no way you could have manifested anything. You were nowhere near bliss.

Then the whisper became louder. You heard God, "You don't have to do it alone, I'll carry you. Just know that I am here, talk to me. I am always with you."

And so, you realized that you did not have to carry it all yourself. You did not have to shit rainbows as you were on your way to bliss, but you you sure as hell knew you were going to get there.

You began to fill your toolkit - with the law of manifestation....intention. Then the second – speaking it as if it is; then, third, you take steps in faith. You learned to embrace the beautiful mess of the struggle that you were in, and you stopped pushing against it.

Through your struggle, you were forced to walk the talk. You see, it's easy to speak of something excitedly and passionately, telling others to wake up and live when we feel good, but how true are you to the whispers of your soul when you're in the trenches? Do you forget God?

You found that you gained a greater appreciation of your strength. You learned to pull yourself up by the bootstraps.

Emotionally, you fell face-first in the mud. You hid in the bushes. You tried to play dead, but the sun rose. You are on your two feet again. You may still be unsure of life, but you are standing.

You learned something powerful. You shed the kryptonite – which was the belief that you couldn't do it. You shed your old skin and it was painful. You let go of myself, and in her place, was someone who no longer needed a cape. You are now walking with Spirit and you remind yourself daily, "Spirit lives inside of me".

You learned to appreciate the struggle, through which the butterfly makes that beautiful transformation. Imagine if someone had helped the butterfly in the transition. That might have ruined the wings.

How else would you have learned life if you didn't live it? How could you speak of the beauty of transformation if you hadn't been there? How else would you know that you were not alone when you felt it? How else would you have believed in magic?

How else would you have learned to appreciate others in their struggle, without having to jump in and rescue. You don't have to fix. Struggle isn't a sin.

You learned to live in the Spirit. You learned to live in the strength-formation.

For in the struggle is where new life begun.

# A PRAYER TO INHALE AND EXHALE, MINDFULLY

My prayer for you is this….

That you remember to be aware of the air…

The air that you breathe into your lungs, the air that you breathe into your life, and the air that you collect through the people in your life.

Air is one thing that we take for granted, but without it, we don't have life.

Today, think about the air you are breathing, the people you, breathe with and the power in how that energy affects your life.

Today, every time you breathe in, actuality and metaphorically, pray for discernment and pray for strength.

Inhale mindfulness, exhale distraction.

Inhale self control and exhale scatteredness.

Inhale peace and exhale worry.

Inhale joy and exhale pain.

Inhale assuredness and exhale doubt.

Inhale that you already have the win.

Inhale the answer.

Inhale the way.

Inhale the knowledge.

Inhale your magnificent birthright.

Inhale the knowledge that you are your own salvation.

Inhale a new you – with new eyes that see the light; a new mouth that speaks only truth; new hands that do only good; and a renewed spirit that manifests all that your soul desires to express through you.

# A PRAYER TO FIND BEAUTY IN LIFE

I've learned a long time ago that what you look for in others and experiences is what you find… Today, my prayer is that you find beauty within each person you meet….

Each human being is a myriad of complexities – woven together from joy, pain, what they have been taught and what they can't even remember being taught.

We accept the idea of our self as "me", but is it really?

Close your eyes and look within. Imagine that no one can hear or see you or your thoughts. Imagine that no one is watching. Who and where would you be?

Remember that you are magic.
Remember that you are made of the stars.
Remember that you are blameless.
Remember that today is the start.

Remember that each breath you take is a new beginning.
Remember that with each exhalation, you can let go.

Remember that you are a soul living in a human body. You are not the sum of your body. You are endlessly more. Endless.
Remember that you chose to be here. So, only you choose what to make with this journey.
Remember that you are pure love. Manifest purity and love in everything.
Remember that you are energy. You were born with this energetic connection through which you are interwoven in with everything.

Remember that every day is a day to dream new dreams.
Remember that in every moment, you can end the old and start new again.
Remember that life is more than your circumstances.
Remember that only you hold the key.

Remember to hold the vision.
Remember to believe.
Remember to create more days when you laughed so hard you can barely breathe.
Remember to look at the world with wonder and hope.

Remember that you are the epiphany. You are the transformation. You are the key.

# A PRAYER FOR KNOWING GOD

Today, I pray...

That you know God. That you know that you have the limitless, unyielding, brilliant, radiant, supportive, protective love of God all around you. Say, in acknowledgement, "Amen".

With excitement, I pray that you relish this amazing, endless love that awaits your every thought, word and move. Say, in enthusiasm, "Amen".

With power, I pray that you see with spiritual eyes, all the previously unseen forces surrounding you, at your fingertips, and that you can bring to life with the power of your tongue. Say, in strength, "Amen".

With gratitude and a full heart, consider the every detail that God has painstakingly and lovingly taken to craft, shape, plan, orchestrate, compose and bring to fruition in your life. Say, in thankfulness, "Amen".

With master artistry, know that you create every aspect of your life, that it is a beautiful, bright, exciting, joy-filled, adventurous, canvas. Every aspect of it – from every blink, to every breath, to every desire, to every manifestation – it was all designed by you. Say, in masterfulness, "Amen".

With comfort, know that there are no stronger, safer arms to protect and guide you. That God's loving embrace enfolds you ever so gently. You are fully loved and always guided. You are never alone. Say, in protection, "Amen".

With beauty, relish every single thing that you lay your eyes on, everything you touch. See the world again like a child and bask in the infinite and myriad gorgeous creations that fill your world. Say, in wonder, "Amen".

With faith, know that your every step is already prepared for, your every joy is already anticipated, your every supply is already filled, your every healing is already manifested, your every dream is already a reality, and your every wish has already appeared. Say, in knowing, "Amen".

With every fiber of your being, believing that God is all, and all is God, say, "It is already done."

# A PRAYER TO KNOW THAT YOU ARE LIMITLESS

Today, my prayer for you is this… that you know you are limitless.

My prayer for you is to know that you are the human droplet that change the course of the world.

My prayer for you is that you recognize that you have the power to create inside of you.

Imagine the wonder of you, all of you. Before you were born, you were limitless, and your limitless soul chose to fill a human body and bring it to life.

Before you were composed of conscious thought, do you know what you were? You were limitless.

Before you had a belief of what you could and couldn't do, you were limitless.

Before you began to tell yourself to accept life as it is, and that you've done the best you could, you were limitless.

Before you grew from a fetus, into a baby, a child, then into an adult, you were limitless.

Before you decided that you weren't enough, you were limitless.

Before you accepted the confines of your world, you were limitless.

Before that person broke your heart, your love was limitless.

Before you made those mistakes, your faith in yourself was limitless.

Before you felt ashamed, pride in your actions was limitless.

Before you told yourself that you didn't have the talent to do that, your capabilities were limitless.

Before you closed your mind to other options, your choices were limitless.

Before you began beating up on yourself, your love for yourself was limitless.

Before you forgot that you could harness the power of God, your matrix was limitless.

Before you stopped talking to your angels, your spiritual support was limitless.

Close your eyes, and go back to that place, from whence you cometh.

Go back to that place beyond your current life.

Go back to that place, before the birth canal squeezed you into this one viewpoint of life.

Go back.

Feel what is was like to be limitless.

Rest in that space a while.

Say to yourself, "I am limitless".

"I am limitless".

"I am limitless".

"I am limitless".

"I am limitless".

"I am limitless".

Now, open your eyes.

From today on, live as a spiritual being in your human body, with no limits.

You are Divinity. You are the ethos. You are all there is.

You are limitless.

# A PRAYER FOR UNVEILING YOUR LIGHT

Before you begin to judge yourself about the decisions you made, know that all of your choices were the right ones at the time you made them.

By taking the time to just be with and in yourself, you can begin to unveil a light to shine on all of the corners of your life that were hidden from you.

Nourish your soul by allowing the darkness to disappear so that with clear eyes you can perceive that beauty and aliveness of life happening right here and right now.

In all moments of your life, this aliveness was always present and you have been interacting with it.

Have the courage now to step up and be tested by the trials that your soul must go through to evolve.

By allowing yourself to make mistakes you begin the path towards enlightenment.

This process is not always a pretty one, but a journey of allowing resistance to exist as you persevere towards your greatness.

You are meant for greatness!

This can only be achieved through becoming a master of your inner world. Be patient in the pursuit of what your sets your soul on fire.

When in your heart you know that you are ready, Unveil your Light and shine it upon the universe!

Be untouchable, unstoppable and unapologetically you!

# A PRAYER TO AWAKEN THE DIVINE FEMININE IN YOU

Your body is a sacred temple.

Only light and love can enter within.

Your spiritual DNA is holy – It has been passed on by generations of light beings that came to life.

Forget not from where you came. You are nature's greatest miracle, sprung from the woman's womb.

The Divine Feminine is within you now, powerful and abundant. It's energy is one that comes from inclusivity, harmony, beauty and love. It's nectar so sweet and nutrient it can bring life even to the most dark. May the power of the divine feminine reveal itself within your heart. Let it's flame ignite the passion and courage to celebrate the miracle of life each day.

Say to yourself, "I love myself. I am not ashamed. I am a Goddess. I am Earth and Mother Earth is Free".

Hear the Divine Feminine call from deep within you, to awaken. She calls on you to rise, and ignite the fire in the sacred temple. As you allow the Divine Feminine phoenix to rise, you may allow yourself to vibrate higher and higher.

In this vibration you find yourself filled with healing and strength. Your creative abilities and capacity to manifest grows.

With deep gratitude, I bow down to you Divine Goddess.

Awaken into your temple.

# A PRAYER TO THE WOMB OF COMPASSION

In our mother's womb, where you were first nurtured, loved, and embraced, you felt connected, and safe.

As you moved into new phases of growth, you slowly started to forget this pure connection with deep compassion and love.

You began to believe that we were truly alone, individual, separated.

You began to believe that you were alone.

You may have become hardened towards yourself and others.

You found some aspects of yourself growing cold to life.

You forgot the soft, warm, supple places. You forgot compassion, deep love and truth - but what is true cannot stay buried, and one day the questions welled up and rose inside of you.

"Why am I really here?"
"Who am I at my core?'
"What is this all for?"

These questions lead you back to where you came from - the womb of compassion, ensconced in warm, love and peace. They remind you to see the pure connection you have with all living things. They fill you with self love, while inspiring you to give that love to others. They remind you to feel again- connected, softer, warmer, deeper. They bring you back to the core of life.

The Womb of Compassion is Always with You.

# A PRAYER TO DEEPEN YOUR EXPERIENCE OF GRATITUDE

Here is a Prayer for you to use to deepen your experience of **Gratitude**.

**Today I woke up** and felt a pure joy flush through my body.

This joy is happiness to be *ALIVE*.

Thank you, **Universe,** for aligning to keep me here alive and thriving today.

**Thank you**, Universe, **for** another day, and **another chance** to live in my highest self.

**Thank you,** Universe for always taking care of my friends, family, loved ones, and I.

Thank you, Universe, **for the fire you burn in my heart.**

**Today, I will focus** on that which is true in my heart so that I may manifest what serves me and the good of all.

Thank you, Universe, for giving me the strength to align and focus **on the path that serves the greater good.**

**Universe,** I become available to you as an open vessel to receive and emit your compassion and grace.

Today **I will keep myself** in the present moment, knowing that whatever arises and subsides is perfect just the way it is.

Universe, **in the quietude of my soul**, I thank you most of all for your unconditional and eternal love.

**Thank you, Thank you, Thank you,
Sincerely, Me**

# A PRAYER TO SEE THE BEAUTY IN YOUR EVERYDAY LIFE

**Before you read on, take a deep breath and become aware that the beauty and intelligence that surrounds you is** *a reflection of self.*

> May your day be filled by the inspiration of the sun
> and your heart bathed by the light of the moon.

> May you see a flower today and explore the depth of its
> simplistic beauty and know in your most pleasant and aware
> state, that it is like you - fresh, alive and peaceful.

> As the seasons change on the earth's surface, may
> you indulge in rest and deep reflection.
> May the changing seasons allow you to understand that
> what is ahead is so much greater than the past.

Cleanse your eyes with the love of the ocean and soar as
high as eagles in the pursuit of your goals and dreams.

Know that when darkness hits the earth, the
moon light is there to guide you home.
Don't let the darkness of the world dim your light because
in this very moment you are meant to Shine.

May you be nestled with all of the beauty nature provides and
know that as you breathe in, the trees around you breathe out.

Synchronized and One with the Entire Universe and Beyond.

With Pure Love and the Bliss of a Hundred Hugs.

# A PRAYER FOR BLESSINGS

May you feel blessed in the midst of all the challenges, for they nourish your growth.
May you stay positive among those who do not see their own light yet, for you become a guiding force by being truly yourself.
May you see the inner being of each individual you interact with today as yourself and listen with compassionate ears.
May you remember your interconnectedness with all that is.
May you know the aliveness of your soul rather than your surface reflection so that you may actualize your true purpose, experiencing it blissfully everyday.
May you anchor yourself to the bedrock of love which is the foundation of all that is, allowing yourself to be in the glory of who you really are.
May you remember that it's never too late to change the program imprinted in your childhood and in your genes from your present or past life.
May you accept yourself completely; this will open the door to change.

May you lovingly support yourself through the process of shifting your experience by being lovingly mindful and tender with the process of your self growth.

May you remember that you cannot solve any problem with hatred, blame, envy, guilt or stress.

May you see your problems as blessings on your path so that your obstacles become only ripples in the vastness of the ocean.

May you see the blessings of the perfectly Divine order unfolding in your daily life.

May you look through the eyes of faith and true humbleness to know that all that you desire and require at this time is right at your fingertips.

May you have real and authentic conversations with your friends and loved ones to build deep and fulfilling connections.

May you have the courage to let go of anything that does not serve you at this time to make more room for what the universe is sending to you.

May you release any thoughts that slow you down or keep you heavy in sorrow, guilt, anger or depression.

May you pay attention to what brings you peace.

May you remember that only your own self-realization can you help others by lifting them into your light.

May you be able to take full responsibility of your life by owning yourself and knowing that you have the strength and ability to respond to anything that comes your way, 'negative' or 'positive'.

Finally, May you remember the entrance to your sanctuary is inside of YOU.

Sending blessings for a positive day, filled with love, laughter and truth.
Sending blessings to your family.
Sending blessings of prosperity.
Sending blessings for good health and vitality.
Sending blessings to find your blissful purpose.
Sending blessings along your journey.
Sending Blessings on Blessings on Blessings!
With GodSpeed,
Amen

# AN AUTHENTIC PRAYER FOR THE DAY

Today, I woke up and I thought...

Today better be fucking different from yesterday.
Today, I don't want anyone to fucking treat me like shit.
Today, may all my fucking problems be gone.
Today, I don't have time for anyone's shit.
Today, let no one fucking cut me off in traffic.
Today, let dudes make up their fucking minds.
Today, don't let any fucking thing bother me.
Today, let me be fucking filled with grace.
Today, God, make it so that at no point in my day should I wonder why the fuck "this" is happening to me.
Today, let life be fucking amazing.

Today, is going to be fucking brilliant.
Today, I look like a fucking million bucks.
Today, I am fucking smart as shit.
I will manifest the fucking hell out of today.
Is anyone going to stop me? Nope. Fuck that.
Today, anything that comes up against me is fucked.

I feel a smile expand across my face.
I exhale.
Fuckin' A. Let this fucking awesome day begin.

Nama-fuckin'-ste!

Maimah Karmo is a spiritual teacher, speaker, author and life coach. *She has also been featured* on *The Oprah Winfrey Show, OWN Good Morning America and the Today Show.* Most dear to her heart is her daughter, Noelle. Maimah publishes Bliss Magazine, hosts *The Pure Bliss* podcast and the "**Manifest**" Conference. Visit www.maimah.com and follow her on Instagram @maimahkarmo.

Tania Koulakian is an entrepreneur, Fitness and Wellness Educator and the Founder of Harmonize, a wellness lifestyle instagram page whose mission is to inspire a life of harmony. At a young age, Tania was naturally curious about spirituality and she questioned life and destiny very often. Always feeling a little different from the crowd she fell a prisoner of her own mind, falling deep into anxiety and depression. Her passion for wellness led her to practicing yoga for many years, deepening her connection to her self and the present moment. She later became a yoga instructor, which helped her realize her true potential to live, grow and keep nourishing the spiritual aspects of her life. This sense of empowerment through her discovery helped her assert that living the life she loves is possible, it just takes nourishing and feeding the genius within. www.harmonize.world Instagram: @harmonize.world